THE CC

For the Body and the Soul

Pamela A. Major

THE COMFORT: FOR THE BODY AND THE SOUL

Publisher Diligence Publishing Company
P.O. Box 2476
Bloomfield, New Jersey 07003

To contact the author to speak at your organization, seminar, or conference see contact information in "about the author" section of this book.

THE COMFORT: FOR THE BODY AND THE SOUL

ISBN: 978-1-7374840-7-3

Printed in the United States

Interior and Cover photos: Shannon Davis Photography

DEDICATION

To my parents...how you showed me love... I can still feel yours. And to all my family, biological, community, and spiritual; your impact has shaped me and allowed me to pour out the love you gave to me into these recipes. I thank you, I cherish you, and I love you...

P.A.M.

Englewood Public Library
To the place where
I practiced research and
increased humility. Thank you
to every staff member who helped
me find everything ♡

PM

4/10/22

TABLE OF CONTENTS

INTRODUCTION

2 Corinthians 1:3-5

3 Praise be to the God and Father of our Lord Jesus Christ, the Father of compassion and the God of all comfort, 4 who comforts us in all our troubles, so that we can comfort those in any trouble with the comfort we ourselves receive from God. 5 For just as we share abundantly in the sufferings of Christ, so also our comfort abounds through Christ.

Healing – *the process of becoming sound or healthy again; (etymology) health, sound, whole*

I have been broken. For many of you reading this, life took some shots and it turned you in directions you could not imagine. It certainly did so for me.

Now the issues I struggle with may not be yours, but each of us, each one of us has something, some area of struggle that begs to become whole. "The Comfort" shares one of the most significant challenges I faced.

I think that the amazing thing about God is in submitting to Him, I found that He took me through a process and like a patient in rehab, I didn't quite know when it happened...I just knew I was better.

It took a long while for me to recognize what was happening, and I know that's okay, what I also know is that the love of God reached me in places and ways that I don't know if I can properly articulate. I know that I am loved deeply by God the Father. This is a rich, deep, inexplicable, and bottomless love.

Ephesians 3:18-19 (NKJV)
18 may be able to comprehend with all the saints what is the width and length and depth and height— 19 to know the love of Christ which passes knowledge; that you may be filled with all the fullness of God.

I find the love of God comforting. His love does not promise a pain free life, that is not what life is; he warns us that there will be issues and complications in this life. What God promises is presence. It is not an overwhelming presence, or one that "feels" the same way all of the time. It is a presence that is available, even waiting for you and me to pull on it (make a demand if you will) and say "Daddy-God, I need you!" in a whisper or a scream, He hears us, and we are helped.

"The Comfort" is my journey, my process through the most devastating time of my life. My journey is mine, but I know that some elements and principles will hit home and you too will realize you are in a process to healing

This book is a prayer. A prayer that in sharing my journey to healing, that it will encourage others to take the journey... receive ***The Comfort***.

THE BASICS – BEFORE YOU GET STARTED

Here are some basics we are adding just as reminders/FYI when cooking:

- PLEASE read the ingredient list carefully BEFORE you get started.
- Soups are usually a combination of leftovers; after you get these down, perhaps you will create your own wonderful blends of bits and pieces.
- Since these soups ARE NOT made from bits and pieces, read the recipes and their components closely, see how you can break them down day by day and put them together on the day you want the soup to be served.
- Consider making a soup in phases, if you cook the components (like sausage or collard greens) in advance, you basically just put them in the pot afterwards.
- NEVER use ingredients you/guests/family are allergic to in order to satisfy our recipes. Experiment and replace ingredients as needed
- If you are on a sensitive diet, use the substitutes utilized in your regular cooking
- ALWAYS Use appropriate heating, cooking, and cooling instructions so your food stays healthy. Cooking your food

to the right internal temperature and cooling it is a must. https://www.fsis.usda.gov/wps/portal/fsis/topics/food-safety-education/get-answers/food-safety-fact-sheets/safe-food-handling/safe-minimum-internal-temperature-chart/ct_index

- TOOLS-
    - at least 1-1.5-gallon stock pot
    - whisk, blender (traditional or immersion)
    - small containers (I prefer glass) for prep (onions, peppers etc.)
    - large, slotted serving spoon
    - regular large (closed bowl) serving spoon
    - serrated knife
    - measuring cups
    - measuring spoons
    - food/freezer safe containers
    - ladle
    - food thermometer

- Enjoy and experiment – cooking should, after all, be fun!

GOOD STOCK

Essentially, stock/broth is easy! It's about good ingredients and time. Here's our list of musts:

- Water
- Celery
- Carrots
- Green Peppers
- Red Peppers
- Garlic
- Bay leaf
- Black Peppercorns
- Major Savour Classic or Caribe
- Major Savour Majormatics
- Cheesecloth

Save some time and make more than one stock at the same time. Make one in a large slow cooker and one or two more on the stove.

Except for RC's Chili, all the soups need a broth/stock. Now I am not fussy about the amounts of ingredients in the stock, but here are some guidelines:

Vegetable Stock – 2-4 carrots and stalks of celery, 4 cloves fresh or roasted garlic, 1-2 red peppers, 1-2 green peppers, 5 bay leaves and 1 teaspoon of black peppercorns (I wrap the bay leaves and peppercorns in cheesecloth and pot them in the pot – all of the flavor, none of the residue), add ¾ gallon of water, 1 tablespoon of salt, 1 tablespoon Major Savour Classic and ½ tablespoon Majormatics.

Turkey Stock – 2-4 carrots and stalks of celery, 4 cloves fresh or roasted garlic, 1-2 red peppers, 1-2 green peppers, 5 bay leaves and 1 teaspoon of black peppercorns (I wrap the bay leaves and peppercorns in cheesecloth and pot them in the pot – all of the flavor, none of the residue), add ¾ gallon of water, 1 tablespoon of salt, 1 tablespoon Major Savour Classic and the turkey carcass.

Chicken Stock (Curry) – 2-4 carrots and stalks of celery, 4 cloves fresh or roasted garlic, 1-2 red peppers, 1-2 green peppers, 5 bay leaves and 1 teaspoon of black peppercorns (I wrap the bay leaves and peppercorns in cheesecloth and pot them in the pot – all of the flavor, none of the residue), add ¾ gallon of water, 1 tablespoon of salt, 1 tablespoon Major Savour Caribe, 1 tablespoon curry and the chicken carcass

Salmon Stock – 1 pound of salmon, 2-4 carrots and stalks of celery, 4 cloves fresh or roasted garlic, 1-2 red peppers, 1-2 green peppers, 5 bay leaves and 1 teaspoon of black peppercorns (I wrap the bay leaves and peppercorns in cheesecloth and pot them in the pot – all of the flavor, none of the residue), add ¾ gallon of water,1 tablespoon of salt, 1 tablespoon Major Savour Classic, 1 teaspoon Majormatics (half in the stock/half in the glaze), 2 tablespoons honey, 1 tablespoon brown sugar. Mix honey, brown sugar, and half of the Majormatics, sprinkle a little salt and Major Savour Classic on the salmon, pour the mixture over the salmon and let rest for an hour. Cut the salmon in half, roast half (about 10-12 minutes at 450 degrees-remove from the stove and allow to rest. Flake salmon and add to the soup as stated in the recipe) and put the other half in the stock pot. Cook stock on a low flame for at least 2 hours (4 hours is preferable).

Shrimp Stock (Curry) -- 1 cup of shrimp shells, 2-4 carrots and stalks of celery, 4 cloves fresh or roasted garlic, 1-2 red peppers, 1-2 green peppers, 5 bay leaves and 1 teaspoon of black peppercorn, s ((I wrap the bay leaves and peppercorns in cheesecloth and pot them in the pot – all of the flavor, none of the residue – placing the shrimp shells in cheesecloth will help make things easier as well), add ¾ gallon of water, 1 tablespoon of salt, 1 tablespoon Major Savour Caribe, 1 tablespoon Curry.

Smoked Turkey Stock – 1-2 smoked turkey drumsticks OR wings, 2-4 carrots ***and*** stalks of celery, 4 cloves fresh or roasted garlic, 1-2 red peppers, 1-2 green peppers, 5 bay leaves and 1 teaspoon of black peppercorns (I wrap the bay leaves and peppercorns in cheesecloth and pot them in the pot – all of the flavor, none of the residue), add ¾ gallon of water, 1 tablespoon of salt, 1 tablespoon Major Savour Classic; you can use this meat for texture in other stews or soups (like Birthright).

SUB-GGESTIONS

Sub-ggestions (Substitutes that could work/things we suggest)

- Swap out cauliflower for potatoes (Glazed Salmon soup).
- If you want smoky flavor without meat, try using sesame oil – just a little, the flavor is potent.
- Use your favorite salt replacement seasonings if you are trying to reduce salt intake.
- Prep soup in stages; a little bit over time will be most effective.
- If you prefer an oil other than olive oil, go ahead and use it.
- Get some freezer safe containers and package soup; this is a great way to prep for lunch.

THE BEGINNING...

The choice of calling this the beginning is to say, I have to pick a start time. The time I chose is when I moved into my first apartment. For many reasons, this was an extreme relief. It was not just about independence; it was an escape.

When you have your own dwelling place, you get to set the rules; I was ready to set my own rules. I did.

My parents were both excited for me and nervous – "was she ready to do this on her own?"

I don't know that I was, but I knew that I had to try. I knew I could go back home, but I did not want to use that option.

Not long after I moved out, my parents started to experience illness, and it was illness at a new level. My father had several eye surgeries, and he was the only driver in the home. My commute became six days a week; five days for work and one day to help out my parents.

As my father started to heal, my mother became ill. She had some dark demons, and I will leave it there. Her story is hers to share; I will just share what I experienced in her dark moments.

Anyone who knew my mother, knew how deeply she loved and what a magnificent person she was (and remains) to me and countless others. I share it more for others who think/are

I am much more careful of these thoughts now. I self-check my words often, words lead someplace. They are not idle, and they all have a temperature. Words are master keys that can lead to destruction or destiny; even the words said inside your head, and especially the words you speak to yourself. Speak well.

Birthright

Savoury and Textured

A reminder that family can always reconcile!

BIRTHRIGHT

The Recipe

Ingredients:

1 bag (16-ounce) of your favorite lentils – dry

½ gallon smoked turkey stock

16 ounces smoked turkey pulse (see stock chapter)

1 can (28 ounces) of crushed tomatoes

1 cooked smoked turkey drumstick OR large wing (see stock chapter)

½ cup of your favorite ketchup

4 ounces sun-dried tomatoes

2 tablespoons of your favorite mustard

1 tablespoon Major Savour Caribe

2 teaspoons salt

¼ cup finely diced onion

¼ cup finely diced green pepper

¼ cup finely diced red pepper

1.5 tablespoons olive oil

Getting to it:

- Clean/Wash the beans with water and check the beans for debris (sometimes a small stone finds its way in).
- Place half of ketchup, mustard, salt, and Major Savour Caribe in a bowl with the beans.
- Pour enough smoked turkey stock to cover beans, cover bowl and refrigerate overnight (or at least four hours).
- In a 1.5-gallon stock pot, put the olive oil, onion and peppers over a flame and allow the mixture to cook (covered) until onions are translucent.
- Uncover pot and put in beans, smoked turkey, sun-dried tomatoes, and the balance of all of the spices, salt, ketchup, and mustard.
- Stir the mixture to make sure the ingredients are coated with the seasonings, ketchup, and mustard.
- Pour in the rest of the stock, make sure there are 2 inches of liquid above the beans (use water to make up the difference if necessary).
- Cook over a medium flame for 1.5 hours, stir occasionally.
- Taste the stock and re-season to taste.
- Cook until the beans are soft (another 1.5 hours...maybe more depending on the beans).
- Makes about 18 (10-ounce) servings.

Birthright Recipe Notes:

Birthright Recipe Notes:

R.C.'s Chili

Hearty and Lush

Have fun in the kitchen and teach those you love!

R.C.'s Chili

The Recipe

Ingredients:

4 pounds ground turkey

½ tablespoon Major Savour-Caribe

1.5 tablespoons salt

2 tablespoons chili powder

1.5 teaspoons chili flakes

1.5 tablespoons of your favorite mustard

3.5 tablespoons honey

2 packages of your favorite chili seasoning mix

1 can (40 ounces) dark red kidney beans

1 can (28 ounces) of diced tomatoes

1 tablespoon olive oil

¼ (each) finely chopped onion, green pepper, and red bell pepper

Getting into it:

- Prep all of your seasonings and vegetables.
- Put oil and vegetables into your pot on a low flame and cover; the onions will become translucent in about 10 minutes.
- Season meat with half the chili powder, honey, mustard, and all other dry seasonings and mix with hands (thoroughly).
- When onions are translucent, place all the meat in the pot and sprinkle the rest of the chili powder over the meat. Mix with a sturdy spoon.
- Break up the meat with the spoon until it is in about 1–2-inch chunks.
- When ground turkey is cooked, add kidney beans, diced tomatoes, and chili seasoning. Cook for another 30 minutes.
- Add crushed tomatoes and let cook for another hour (or two if you can. Time is chili's best friend).
- Yields 16 (10 ounce) servings (freezes well).

R.C.'s Chili Recipe Notes:

R.C.'s Chili Recipe Notes:

Coconut Curry Chicken

In honor of my heritage!

Coconut Curry Chicken

The Recipe

Ingredients

4 chicken thighs

1.5 cups petite carrots

3 lbs. red potatoes (cleaned and cut into 1-inch cubes (I leave the skin on. Do what works for you.)

½ gallon curry chicken stock (or add 1 tablespoon Major Savour Caribe and 1 tablespoon curry powder to chicken stock)

1.25 cups olive oil

1 cup all-purpose flour

13.5 ounces coconut milk

¼ cup onion

¼ cup green pepper

¼ cup red pepper

2.5 teaspoons salt

1 tablespoon curry

1.5 tablespoons Major Savour Caribe

1 teaspoon cayenne pepper

Let's get into it:

- Use Curry Stock recipe to create your stock and cook your chicken.
- When stock is complete, pull chicken apart into shreds and remove all bones. Set aside chicken and allow to cool properly and then refrigerate.
- Sauté onions and peppers (about 12 minutes) on a medium flame.
- When the onions are translucent, turn the flame to low/medium.
- Add carrots, seasonings, and stock. Add the potatoes after about fifteen minutes.
- When vegetables are just about fork tender, create your slurry.
- Slurry – While soup is cooking mix flour and oil in a separate pan, stirring often (like making a roux.) When thoroughly mixed and smooth, add coconut milk and continue to stir constantly.
- Add chicken to the stock pot and cook for 5 minutes.
- Add slurry to the soup and allow to cook another 10-15 minutes.
- Yields 12 (10 ounce) servings.

Coconut Curry Chicken Recipe Notes:

Coconut Curry Chicken Recipe Notes:

YOU MAKE IT

The death of my parents changed my world. We were a tight little unit. We were closed, no insulated. We had our humor, rituals and of course shorthand. My parents had their human failings, but I am amazed how they chose to break with traditions. They, in many ways, knew how to "eat the meat and spit out the bones" of their own upbringings. They were clued in on parenting and while they would not call it a mission statement, they were determined to "raise a decent human being." Mission accomplished!

My mother was the first to die. What made her death more challenging was people kept saying, "I am so sorry to hear about your father." You see my father had major heart surgery and had a stroke on the operating table. When people heard about the death, they assumed it was my dad, but it was my mom. It's not uncommon. She was already suffering in her body. The stress of caring for my father and wondering how he would be, I think took the final toll on her – she was never good at (what we call) self-care.

When I got the news from my father (he called and said, "She's gone. Your mother's gone)," my organizer's mind took over. I packed clothing, made sure everything was shut down and hit the road for home and to see my father. How he must have felt losing the love of his life...

It was challenging, but we muddled through the arrangements and began the pursuit of this life without Mom.

We weren't quite together when the other shoe dropped. My father joined my mother. While I was certainly relieved that the pain he endured was over (he was recovering from bypass surgery and an emotional broken heart), I was now (in my mind) totally alone.

In my core, I felt abandoned and afraid. Much of my family was geographically far away. Those who were close had so much going on, they were unable to spend a great deal of time with us, with me. I felt alone and uncovered.

My family was small, but mighty and tight. Even with illness and issues, we were close, and I always felt their protection, and then they were gone, and I didn't know I was asking the question, "Who will cover me now?" Perhaps somewhere hidden in you, the same question is being asked; maybe you've been asking this question for a very long time. I offer this answer, God the Father will cover you. I hope reading this story will convince you to allow Him to cover your life.

The first of the mechanical and numb years looked okay, prosperous even. I inherited two homes, sold one and then purchased a townhome. I sold the second and THOUGHT it was enough to help me become a full-time entrepreneur. It probably was, but my plan was so flimsy, it just didn't hold up; like I said, I was mechanical and numb.

The details are dull, but the impact was mighty. My financial mismanagement led me into a state of homelessness. I never slept in my car or under a bridge, but I did not have my own residence and no matter how you slant it, that's homeless. I couldn't get any assistance because I do not have children – isn't that something? (One child was the difference between assistance and abandonment, and it still remains the same.)

I did not imagine my life having this chapter...I was homeless. It taught me lessons, it made me vulnerable, it made me humble, and it built my faith.

For some of that time, I lived in the home of an associate, someone who was close to a close friend who could not house me. It was a great favor on both their parts. I am grateful for the open door; there were so many more tragic ways to be homeless. I had my own room in a very comfortable suburban town with my own bathroom, closet, satellite television and more. It sounds like a dream, but each night on my pillow I thought to myself, *"You are without a home."*

I was not working; rather I was not employed. I left a very comfortable job for the discomfort of entrepreneurship. It was exciting and thrilling. The bills kept coming and my plan was more "pie in the sky" than strategic. I could give you many more details, but the bottom line is I lost something that for me stabilizes and provides safety – a home.

I could give you a timeline of the events that took place, but in fact my feelings and thoughts around it are a blur. What I do know is, I understand what it is like to not have your own. I understand the feeling of hopelessness and helplessness when you in the words of the character Blanche DuBois say, "I've always depended on the kindness of strangers." This is a humility that is quite excruciating in nature, being at the mercy/benevolence of others is a lot to endure. There is no telling when that mercy will change, no telling.

I was out of place and without the people who always gave me the support I needed, the support I desired, my parents.

Loss is as multi-layered as an onion, as multifaceted as a gem, and as intricate as a maze. Trauma is a funny thing –

often you don't know you are experiencing it. Something on the inside flips a switch and you just act differently, your responses have altered, and you consciously think of it as okay. Now this is NOT clinical, it's my experience – I see on this side of healing, that I had changed. Sometimes I didn't know how hurt I was until healing began to manifest.

We don't always know the "medicine" or the path that healing takes. My healing came by way of stock, ingredients, seasonings, poultry/seafood, heat, and time. God knew what to use and how to use it in my life. I have come to learn that when you submit to God, He knows the vehicle to use to move you from brokenness to wholeness (shalom).

Cooking was the first thing I asked to learn how to do. I asked my father's mother if she would teach me how to cook. Somewhere in my young (five-year-old) mind, I observed her skill, talent, and ability. She not only could cook well, but people always gathered at her table. Everyone from our family, to old neighbors from New York, to flower club members from her church. Her hospitality drew others; I wanted to have that ability. I knew part of that had to do with the delicious food that happened in that house every day.

Now, my mother was no slouch in the kitchen (ask my friends about her fried shrimp and her friends about her potato salad). My father was also an excellent (albeit messy) cook. They too gathered crowds of friends and family around the table.

In my generation, I had the party house as well. Food was always present at my parties along with a cake or two – I loved it. It is no surprise as I write this, that God would use one of my first loves (cooking and gathering people) as a way to help me heal from this irreplaceable loss. Here's how it happened.

One night when I was not feeling well, I heated up some soup (from a can). I walked across the kitchen and in just a few steps I heard these words, "You make soup." The kitchen has often been a space where I hear (feel strong impressions from) God... you know when you hear His voice. It is clear, it is familiar, and it is certain; quite certain. I responded with these words, "I have two recipes, those that my father gave me; what can I do with that?" (Isn't it funny when we tell God what we have and what little it is – ask the woman with the pot of oil 2 Kings 4:1-7 or the disciples with 2 fish and five loaves John 6/Mark 6).

I ate my soup and went to lay my head on the pillow and POW. Names of soups started to flood my mind. It was so rapid, so incredible, I had to sit up in my bed and start writing (I keep a journal and pen by my bed all the time.) This was the beginning of my soup making era.

I have always been a soup lover, I still am. I never thought I would have all of these original recipes! I also didn't know the real purpose of these soups. I thought they were for others. I didn't know that God had a much deeper and intense use for these soups and that use was to heal me.

I chose the title "The Comfort" because each of us needs to be comforted. Soup with its warmth, flavors and textures fills us up and keeps us full. Soup has a healing quality about it and gives us a feeling of safety and rest. Soup takes bits and pieces, flavors and leftovers and makes something new and wonderful out of what remains.

I wrote the names of the soups in my journal and began the process of praying for recipes. I have to say, they came pretty easily. Sometimes I had to improve my skill/technique, but the recipes came so easily, it's one of those things you realize God gave you – you can't take credit, you just respect what He has provided.

I was not able to move immediately on making the soups, I had research to complete, supplies to purchase and a long list of other to dos. One thing was certain, I was going to make soup.

Coconut Curry Shrimp

More than a memory, a family!

Coconut Curry Shrimp

The Recipe

Ingredients:

2 pounds peeled and deveined shrimp (31-40 or 51-60 count)

3 lbs. red potatoes (cleaned and cut into 1-inch cubes – I leave the skin on. Do what works for you.)

½ gallon curry chicken stock (or add 1 tablespoon Major Savour Caribe and 1 tablespoon curry powder to chicken stock)

1.25 cups olive oil

¼ cup onion

¼ cup green pepper

¼ cup red pepper

2.5 teaspoons salt

1 tablespoon curry

1.5 tablespoons Major Savour Caribe

Let's get into it:

- Season the shrimp with 1 teaspoon of salt along with 1 tablespoon curry and Major Savour Caribe (I would do this the night before). Seal completely and refrigerate overnight or for at least 4 hours.
- In your stock pot, sauté onions and peppers. When the onions are translucent, add the potatoes, seasonings, and stock.
- When potatoes have cooked for about 30 minutes (potatoes should be soft/fork tender.) add shrimp allowing it to cook (pink on both sides about 15 minutes).
- After you add the shrimp, create a slurry.
- Slurry – medium heat – while soup is cooking, mix flour and oil *in a separate pan*, stirring often (like making a roux). When thoroughly mixed and smooth, add coconut milk and continue to stir constantly).
- Add slurry to the soup (slowly) using a spoon or whisk afterward to make sure slurry is totally mixed in and allow to cook another 10-15 minutes.
- Yield – 12 (10 ounce) servings

Coconut Shrimp Recipe Notes:

Coconut Shrimp Recipe Notes:

Dirty Turkey

"Thanksgiving in a bowl"

The joy of family celebrations cannot be underestimated!

Dirty Turkey

The Recipe

Ingredients:

4 turkey thighs

2 packages of hot turkey sausage

1 quart of collard greens

2 cups cooked rice

1 tablespoon Major Savour Classic

1.5 teaspoons salt

1 tablespoon of your favorite vinegar (to use for cooking collard greens – I also suggest cooking using turkey or smoked turkey stock.)

3 tablespoons of butter

2 quarts smoked turkey stock

1 quart turkey stock

Getting into it:

- This soup should be made over the course of two or three days. It has several components, and it will make the final preparation much easier.
- Use turkey thighs from the making of the turkey stock. If you bought the turkey stock, roast turkey thighs covered for about 40-45 minutes – make sure the thighs have an internal temperature (see chart from usda website) before allowing them to cool.
- Pull the meat of the turkey thighs allowing them to cool and then refrigerate. Remove all bones.
- Cook collard greens in 8 ounces of turkey stock and then cover with water; add the vinegar and salt and pepper to taste (throw in half a small onion and green pepper for extra flavor).
- Remove the skin from the turkey sausage. Sauté the turkey sausage breaking it up into crumbles as it sautés. Save as much of the oil from the sausage as possible.
- Remove the sausage from the pot with a slotted spoon (leaving the oil in the pot).
- Pour the rice into the same pot (with the oil from the cooked sausage) and 2 tablespoons of butter. Cover rice with a combination of water and smoked turkey stock making sure the rice is covered with 1-1.5 inches of the mixture.

- Bring rice to a boil and then turn down to low, cooking for 20 minutes. Let cool then refrigerate. The rice goes into the soup at the very last moment.
- Put the olive oil and vegetables into your pot. Allow vegetables to cook until onions are translucent (about 10 minutes).
- Add sausage, pulled turkey thighs, collard greens and turkey stock. Let simmer between low and medium for an hour. Re-season as desired.
- Add rice, stirring it into the soup; allow to cook for another 15-30 minutes (rice absorbs the stock; if it is too thick for you, add more stock or water – taste and re-season).
- Yield – 28 (10 ounce) servings (freezes well)

Dirty Turkey Recipe Notes:

Glazed Salmon

"Smooth Luxury"

Sometimes you just need to be spoiled!

Glazed Salmon

The Recipe

Ingredients:

4 pounds russet potatoes (cleaned, peeled and cut into 1-inch cubes)

1 pound of your favorite salmon

¾ cup of milk

¼ cup brown sugar

¼ cup honey

2 sticks unsalted butter

2 teaspoons salt

2 teaspoons rosemary

2 teaspoons Majormatics

1 quart of salmon stock

1.5 tablespoons olive oil

Getting into it:

- Create your salmon stock (see recipe in good stock section).
- Let the salmon cool and then flake.
- Wash peel and cut potatoes (1-inch cubes).
- Put olive oil and 1 stick of butter, potatoes, and the rest of the seasonings in your pot; stir to make sure all of the potatoes are coated.
- Pour the stock over the potatoes (it should not cover the potatoes. Place cover on stock pot and allow to cook until tender. Taste to re-season.
- Use your favorite blender (I suggest an immersion blender) to mash the potatoes – they don't need to be totally smooth – it should have a rustic mashed potato consistency.
- Add the flaked salmon and the other stick of butter and milk – stir to mix the salmon throughout.
- Let simmer on low for 15-20 minutes; check every few minutes to make sure potatoes don't stick.
- Makes 7 (10 ounce) servings.

Glazed Salmon Recipe Notes:

Glazed Salmon Recipe Notes:

Harvest

"Blended Bliss"

A reminder that what you plant will grow!

HARVEST

The Recipe

Ingredients:

1 bag (22-ounces) diced chicken

1 package (2 large links) smoked turkey sausage

20 ounces mixed vegetables

8 ounces barley

½ gallon smoked turkey stock

½ small onion (diced)

¼ cup red pepper (diced)

¼ cup green pepper (diced)

½ tablespoon salt

1 tablespoon Major Savour Classic

1 tablespoon olive oil

Let's get into it:

- Cut the sausage the long way, then cut the short way into ¼ inch slices.
- Sautee the sausage, onions, and peppers (about 12 minutes).
- Add the vegetables and chicken; stirring all the contents together; let cook for about 5 minutes.
- Add the stock and all the seasonings; stir thoroughly and let cook for 45 minutes over a low to medium heat.
- Add barley and cook for another 20-25 minutes.
- Yield 14 (10 ounce) servings

Harvest Recipe Notes:

Harvest Recipe Notes:

THE JOURNEY

Well, now I had the names and recipes for over 20 soups in addition to the two I inherited from my father. I had some delays due to my living situation, but I finally got back into my own home and I got started with my first few recipes.

I took advantage of what I learned watching cooking shows, family tips, and personal experience. Sometimes it was great and other times, well, my garbage was pretty full!

Honestly, it didn't take too long. I started out with four soups. Two were my dad's (RC's Chili and Russell's Rustic Turkey) and Smoky/Sweet Turkey and Chicken Confetti. I packaged them and let the people know what I was doing.

People loved them!

The soups touched people. It was clear that it was more than the soup, it opened up an emotional place in people. At tastings, people would ask me for the recipe without even knowing it (well, some people knew what they were doing). I would often hear, "I don't like these things, but the way they come together in this soup –delicious."

One of the ways people were pulled in was the names of the soups. It's kind of difficult to ignore something called "Dirty Turkey" or "Glazed Salmon." When you hear names like that, it sparks interest. It was time to get serious.

I got all of the business things completed. There were numerous hurdles, but I managed to clear them. I was ready…maybe.

I started to develop a strategy for growth. I wanted to do online sales. I wanted the feel of home. Yes, I wanted the feeling of receiving a care package from home. I imagined sending handwritten notes and building relationships with people I might never meet. I imagined and then I started to get pulled. It wasn't instant. It was a whisper (initially) – *"There is something else."* As I said earlier, you know when you hear His voice; you just do.

I didn't really want to hear this; I was investing a great deal of time and effort into these soups and the development of a company; and then it happened – questions.

I questioned what I was doing; I questioned if this was the right thing. I questioned how I would manage this business and speaking engagements and encourage others – how could I do it?

The soups were still delicious. There was too much of the "main ingredient" (I'll talk about that later) for them not to be. I still prayed over them and played gospel music over them and asked God to fill in whatever I might have missed in making them. It began to be a chore, it lost something, and I couldn't place what it was; but it was lost.

I began the process of saying and praying, "How do I end this chapter?" God used a dear friend who gave me the idea – "create a cookbook." It was perfect, I could allow the soups to have life, come into countless homes and remove myself from this work. I was ready with a plan!

“Jackson Love”

“Oooh Wee Good Gumbo”

Family is joined by blood and also by selection!

"Jackson Love"

The Recipe

Ingredients:

- 2 links smoked turkey sausage (cooked and cut into ¼ inch slices)
- 2 pounds large shrimp (51-60 count-peeled, cleaned, and deveined)
- 4 chicken thighs (seasoned with Tony Chachere's and (Gumbo) file – cook for 40 minutes at 350 degrees or until juices run clear/internal temperature of 180 degrees.
- ½ gallon smoked turkey stock
- 1 cup chopped celery
- 1 cup chopped green pepper
- 1 large, chopped onion (I prefer Vidalia)
- 1 cup all-purpose flour (feel free to try almond or other flours here.)
- 1 stick unsalted butter
- ½ cup vegetable oil
- ¼ cup balsamic vinegar
- 1 cup chopped okra (fresh or frozen)
- 1 cup shrimp shells

- 3-4 bay leaves
- 1 teaspoon black peppercorn
- 8 ounces tomato paste
- 1.5 tablespoons Tony Chachere's Original Creole Seasoning
- 1.5 teaspoon file
- 1.5 teaspoon pepper flakes OR cayenne pepper
- Cheesecloth (enough to wrap up bay leaves, shrimp shells and peppercorns)

Getting into it:

Prep time (cook sausage and chicken a day or two in advance-season chicken and shrimp with .5 teaspoons each of Tony Chachere's, file and cayenne at the same time). Carefully seal raw shrimp and refrigerate.

Day of 30-40 minutes (chopping vegetables and organizing ingredients)

Cook time – give at least 1 ½ hours of cooking time BEFORE adding the shrimp. Give another 15-30 minutes afterward (check to make sure shrimp is pink/well cooked). Time is gumbo's friend!

- Over a medium flame, put butter and vegetable oil into your stock pot. Once melted, add flour.
- Stir often, roux tends to all of a sudden cook. You want it to be somewhere between the color of peanut butter and chocolate.
- Add onions, celery, and peppers. Cover and allow to sweat for about 15 minutes.
- Add shrimp shells, peppercorns, and bay leaf (in cheesecloth) tomato paste, vinegar, 1 cup of stock and seasonings and cook covered for another 15-20 minutes.
- Add sausage, chicken and the rest of the stock – let cook for another 20 minutes.
- Add shrimp and cook for another 10-15 minutes.
- Yield 10 (10 ounce) servings

“Jackson Love” Recipe Notes:

Roasted Vegetable Melange

“Mixed Magic”

Life brings texture and variety – enjoy!

Roasted Vegetable Melange

The Recipe

Ingredients:

3-4 medium or large sweet potatoes

3 small zucchinis cleaned and cubed (1 inch)

2 yellow squash cleaned and cubed (1 inch)

2 small eggplants cleaned and cubed (1 inch)

1 can (28 ounces) of diced tomatoes

40 ounces vegetable stock

1.5 teaspoons cinnamon

1 tablespoon salt

1.5 tablespoons Major Savour Classic

Getting into it:

- Clean and roast sweet potatoes in a flat pan (that can hold more ingredients) for about 30 minutes at 450 degrees.
- Add the zucchini, squash and eggplant add half tablespoon Major Savour and sprinkle a small amount of the salt, sprinkling it evenly over all of the vegetables. Allow it to continue roasting at 350 degrees for about 15 minutes.
- Remove vegetables from the oven and allow to cool for about 20 minutes or until you are able to handle the sweet potatoes (gloves are HIGHLY suggested when handling the sweet potatoes).
- Cut the sweet potatoes into 1-inch cubes.
- Put all vegetables into the stock/diced tomato mixture.
- Cover and allow to cook for at least 90 minutes.

Roasted Vegetable Melange Recipe Notes:

Roasted Vegetable Melange Recipe Notes:

Russell's Rustic Turkey

The good stuff can come in the leftovers!

Russell's Rustic Turkey

The Recipe

Ingredients

3 quarts turkey stock

1 quart of water

1.5-2 pounds cooked turkey meat

24 ounces mixed vegetables

4 medium sized white or Yukon gold potatoes (I inch cubed and peeled)

¼ cup small, diced onion

¼ cup small diced red pepper

¼ cup small diced green pepper

1.5 cup of ketchup

1.5 teaspoon Sage

1.5 tablespoons Major Savour Classic

2 tablespoons olive oil

1 tablespoon salt

Let's get into it:

- In a 1.5-gallon stock pot, add the olive oil, onions, red and green peppers on medium heat. Cover and allow them to sweat and become translucent.
- Add stock salt, Major Savour, sage, and ketchup and allow to cook for 15 minutes.
- Add mixed vegetables, turkey, and water.
- Taste after allowing to simmer for 20 minutes; re-season as needed.
- Allow to simmer on low for one hour.
- Add diced potatoes and cook until fork tender (15-20 minutes).
- Taste and re-season as needed.
- Serve and be delighted.
- Makes about 9 10-ounce servings.

Russell's Rustic Turkey Recipe Notes:

Russell's Rustic Turkey Recipe Notes:

THE AWAKENING

I had been making soups for a few years. I developed the business and had a wonderful name "The Pampered Pot." I admit a few missteps, but I was beginning to gain traction in the business.

I started to develop a business model, something that made us unique and our product in demand. I began to know my customers (so important) and I knew what they liked. It was starting to work.

I don't remember where I was, I don't remember the day or even the time of day, but I do remember the reality, these soups were a picture of my life. How did I miss that? How did it escape me? The simple answer is, God revealed it to me when I was ready.

I shared throughout this story that the death of my parents devastated me. There is a pain that is so deep a blow to the soul that can be *almost* impossible to recover from. I believe that I was "anesthetized" from that pain. Even so, I took it hard and didn't put the pain in the right places and in the right ways. I built walls and shut down. I was afraid, deathly afraid. I kept (unknowingly) asking the question "who will leave me next?" God took me through a process to reveal to me the pain, after the healing took hold.

I was making progress, I sure looked okay, but up close I was a mess. I kept making the soups and then memories of family and events began to erupt into my memories. It was an internal photo album or family movie. In all, my broken pieces, the flavors and textures of my life were put together in a "pot" placed over some heat and came together as something completely other, something that could nourish and heal others; now I could share healing and the story of my healing with others.

Let me make it a little more clear. Each of these soups has a direct connection to someone(s) or events in my life. Birthright makes me think of my father and his older brother; Dirty Turkey and Russell's Rustic, the family holiday dinner; and White Bean Wonder, family dinners at my grandparents (the Majors). Each soup reminded me of the people I love and the experiences we enjoyed together.

All of a sudden, I could see that God had taken my pain and put it in a pot! He took what I could not say with my mouth and let me share the love I had for all of these people and places (especially my hometown of Englewood, NJ) and he poured out healing balm in the form of soup.

Each time I made one of these soups, I unloaded my grief and shared my love all at the same time.

I wonder, is there something that you do that is expressing "I love you and I miss you" to the world? Could you perhaps be paying tribute to someone or something in your art, hobbies, or another daily habit?

God can use what you love to heal what is broken in your life.

Summer Holiday

"Fun and Flavor"

Bring together your family – biological and otherwise...and have fun!

Summer Holiday

The Recipe

Ingredients:

1 bag (22 ounces) of cooked diced chicken

1 bag (20 ounces) of mixed vegetables

3 ears of fresh corn (roast, cool and cut off the kernels and store in a bowl the day before)

5 medium sized potatoes (cleaned and cut into ½ inch dice)

6 tablespoons barbecue sauce

½ tablespoon Major Savour Classic

2 teaspoons of salt

40 ounces chicken stock

1 pint of water

½ small onion (diced)

1/4 cup red pepper (diced)

¼ cup green pepper (diced)

1.5 tablespoons olive oil

Getting into it:

- Place oil, onions and peppers in stock pot and sauté – low/medium flame until onions are translucent (about 12 minutes).
- Add potatoes, seasonings and half the stock; cook covered for 15 minutes.
- Add roasted corn kernels.
- Add in chicken, seasonings, barbecue sauce and vegetables, then stir thoroughly.
- Cook for another 30 minutes.
- Yield 16 (10 ounce) servings

Summer Holiday Recipe Notes:

Summer Holiday Recipe Notes:

White Bean Wonder

"Creamy and Classic...with a twist"

Good conversation with those you love... priceless!

White Bean Wonder

The Recipe

Ingredients:

1 16-ounce bag dry navy beans

1 16-ounce bag dry great northern beans

½ gallon vegetable stock

½ cup of your favorite ketchup

2 tablespoons of your favorite mustard

1 tablespoon Major Savour Classic

1 tablespoon Majormatics

¼ tablespoon nutmeg

2 teaspoons salt

16 ounces vegetable pulse (see stock chapter)

¼ cup finely diced onion

¼ cup finely diced green pepper

¼ cup finely diced red pepper

1.5 tablespoons olive oil

Getting to it:

- Clean/Wash the beans with water and check the beans for debris (sometimes a small stone finds its way in).
- Place half of ketchup, mustard, salt, and Major Savour Classic in a bowl with the beans.
- Pour enough cooled vegetable stock to cover beans, cover bowl and refrigerate overnight (or at least four hours).
- In a 1.5-gallon stock pot, put the olive oil, onion and peppers over a medium flame and allow the mixture to cook (covered) until onions are translucent (about 12 minutes).
- Uncover pot and put in beans, and the balance of all of the spices, salt, ketchup, and mustard.
- Stir the mixture to make sure the beans are coated with the seasonings, ketchup, and mustard.
- Pour in the rest of the stock, make sure there is at least 2 inches of liquid above the beans.
- Cook over a medium flame for 1.5 hours, stir occasionally.
- Taste the stock and re-season to taste.
- Cook until the beans are soft (another hour...maybe more depending on the beans).
- Makes about 16 (10 ounce) servings.

White Bean Wonder Recipe Notes:

White Bean Wonder Recipe Notes:

THE COMFORT

[3] Blessed be the God and Father of our Lord Jesus Christ, the Father of mercies and God of all comfort, [4] who comforts us in all our tribulation, that we may be able to comfort those who are in any [a]trouble, with the comfort with which we ourselves are comforted by God. 2 Corinthians 1:3-4 NKJV

So we close with this-the comfort. The comfort, for each of us, life brings times when we want to scream, when issues, conflicts and more come to us. Sometimes we have an immediate answer, sometimes we choose well and others not so much. Sometimes we are confused, burdened, and halted. Whatever we are, God the Father is with us-always.

I have come to realize that God, the Father is always with me – ALWAYS. I look at this as the greatest comfort that any of us can have – He is with me and He is with you.

Some question this – If God is with me always, why did He allow this to happen? I can't answer that, but what I can say is this; for every horrible no-good thing, for every potentially heart-stopping moment, He has been with me.

He saw my pain when my parents died. He saw how it shut me down. He saw my fears and anguish. He saw it all. He knew what it would do to me, or rather, the way I would react to their transition. He saw my loneliness. He saw my confusion and the way I could be robotic; He saw how I handled business and fell apart all at the same time. He knew how to bring me through and out – He saw, and He knew.

When I cried on the outside and on the inside, He knew how to "quiet me with His love."

God knew how to use one of my first loves – cooking and soups. He blended them in a wonderful "prescription" to help me heal. He used my childhood and adult memories of wonderful family times and challenging life experiences. He used it all, for "all things work together for the good of those that love the Lord and are called according to his purposes" (Romans 8:28).

I can't begin to know your challenge; I wouldn't try. I also won't minimize or pasteurize your pain. I won't presume to know the proper "prescription" for moving into healing for you – I couldn't, and I wouldn't. What I will do is point you in the direction of a loving Father.

The Father made us and knows us, and greatest of all, loves us. He speaks (impresses, illuminates, and shows) in a way and method unique to each one of us – He does.

For me, it was cooking, for you it could be any of a thousand things.

I know that the Father allows us to experience and grow from pain. He does **NOT** love seeing us in pain, but He also knows that the testing of our faith produces perseverance (James 1:3).

So what is "the comfort?" For me, it was taking my brokenness and loss and using what I love to help me process engineered by WHO I love, my God and Father.

My hope, my prayer, is that whatever your pain, your trauma, or your challenge may be, you too will turn to God, the Father and allow the healing to happen.

Blessings...

The LORD your God in your midst, The Mighty One, will save; He will rejoice over you with gladness, He will quiet you with His love, He will rejoice over you with singing." Zephaniah 3:17

The Best Ingredient

I believe everyone who cooks uses this ingredient.

If you are a professional chef, line cook, caterer, or home cook/food enthusiast – this ingredient is in every dish.

Whether it is sweet or savory, you use it. If it is simple or complex, you use it.

It goes across techniques and cuisines. It applies to multi-step recipes and simple 1-2-3 recipes.

This ingredient suits every kitchen and every pot...

The ingredient is LOVE.

And so we know and rely on the love God has for us.
God is love (I John 4:16a).

ABOUT THE AUTHOR

Pamela A. Major

The Story

Pamela A. Major is an author who infuses healing in everything she writes. Her second book, "The Comfort", gives the readers delicious recipes for the body and shares her story for the healing of her broken heart. "The Comfort" weaves unique soup offerings like Dirty Turkey and Jackson Love with a journey of discovery and soul repair.

The Person

Pamela A. Major is an author, speaker, and life coach. She enjoys seeing her clients become stronger and solidify their space in the market and in the world. She believes "Being yourself is the edge for everyone. Standing out is possible only when the authentic person or organization comes forward.

Major believes the healthier the person, the healthier the community, family, business, and world. "I want to do my part to help bring wholeness to the world. One book at a time, one new belief embraced, we can become better."

Major works as a life success coach with individuals and success strategist with organizations. She also consults with several non-profit organizations. Her first book is ***"I Am A Diamond: Journal and Playbook for Life."***

Booking and Contact Information

Ms. Major can be booked for interviews or appearances through troy.todman@outlook.com

Phone: 732.588.7680

Email: info@meliabloom.com

Website: www.meliabloom.com

ORDER INFORMATION

You can order additional copies of this book by emailing the author directly using the email address below.

Pamela A. Major

Email Address:

info@meliabloom.com

Books are available at Amazon.com, BN.com
Kindle and Your Local Bookstores (By Request)